EXTREME Environments

Deborah Underwood

Contents

Rigby

A Harcourt Achieve Imprint

www.Rigby.com
1-800-531-5015

A World of Extremes

Imagine a mountaintop where plumes of ice grow at the rate of one foot every hour, where you can watch a beautiful ice sculpture form over the course of one day. What about a desert where decades pass without rain, and the ground is dry and cracked in a thousand different places. How could anything possibly live there?

Imagine winds that gust at speeds of 200 miles per hour. Could you survive out in the open with such winds blasting against you? How about temperatures of more than 130° Fahrenheit? What's it like trying to survive in such harsh environments?

Now try to imagine a place that has never seen the sun's rays. This is a place where there is nothing but darkness all day, all year round. What sort of creature could live there? Would it look like anything you've ever seen before?

In this book we'll visit some of Earth's most extreme climates. We'll see why these climates are so difficult to live in, and we'll also check out some of the amazing creatures that call these places their homes. So grab a heavy coat, some sunscreen, an umbrella, and a big water bottle—we need to be ready for anything!

Chapter 1

The Coolest Places on Earth

Got your parka zipped up and your gloves on? Good, because the first stop on our extreme climate tour will be one of the coldest places in the world. We're heading south to the thick ice of Antarctica and then north to the frozen Arctic Sea.

White Worlds

One of the reasons why the North and South Poles stay so cold is because the sun's rays never shine directly on them. Earth is a globe, like a huge ball. When the sun shines on a globe, the rays shine stronger at the middle, the equator, than they do at the top and bottom, the poles.

In fact, the sun's rays are slanted when they reach the poles, and therefore they are not nearly as powerful as those that hit the equator at full force. Since these slanted rays are not as powerful, Earth's atmosphere is able to block out much of the sun's heat. In the end, you get very weak sunrays that don't have the power to heat the poles much above freezing.

Summer at the North Pole

Least Heat

Most Heat

Least Heat

Summer at the South Pole

Least Heat

Most Heat

Least Heat

The angle of the sun's rays has a huge effect on what kind of climate you'll have. Strong, direct rays give you tropical vacations. Weak, slanted rays mean a chilly dip in a sea of ice water.

Earth spins on an axis, but this axis does not run perfectly up and down. It is tilted at 23° to the side. At different times during the year, this tilt is pointed toward the sun, and at others it is tilted away. This means that the poles get sunlight for only part of the year. During the months of June through August, the North Pole tips toward the sun, giving it light and warmth all day and night. During the months of December through February, the Earth has rotated to the other side of the sun. Now the South Pole is tilted toward the sun, which means that it is the one that gets the light. Meanwhile, the North Pole plunges into months of darkness.

The tilt of Earth's axis is always pointed in the same direction. This is why we have seasons and also why Earth's poles get sunlight for only part of the year.

One Extreme Continent

Antarctica definitely takes first prize for Earth's most extreme continent. Not only is it the coldest region on the planet, but it is also the windiest and even the driest! There are no permanent human settlements on Antarctica. Its climate is far too cold for people to live there for more than a few months at a time.

Keeping the Poles Freezing Cold

If you have ever squinted while looking at a bright, snow-covered field, you know that snow reflects the sun's rays really well. Ice and snow keep polar areas freezing cold because they reflect much of the sun's energy before it can heat the ground.

Where does all this ice come from? In the winter many of the polar seas freeze into giant blocks of ice. It takes a long time for these large masses of ice to melt, so most stay frozen all year long. This means that there is always plenty of ice and snow to reflect the sun's warmth away, so the poles stay cold.

Antarctica's strong winds are partly caused by the thick layer of ice—almost three miles thick in some places—that covers the continent. Antarctica is shaped like a dome. The highest point on this dome is at its center, which has an average height of more than 7,500 feet above sea level.

The dome's thick ice chills the air around it. Since cold air sinks and warmer air rises, this super-chilled air rushes down the dome toward the coasts, causing very strong winds. Some places often have 55-mile-per-hour winds, but some 200-mile-per-hour winds have also been recorded.

In July of 1983, Antarctica's Vostok research station, which is about 620 miles from the South Pole, recorded the world's coldest surface temperature ever: -128.6° F. Vostok's average temperature during the winter is -88° F.

Although we often think of deserts as hot places, a desert is actually any place that doesn't get much rainfall. The Sahara Desert in Africa is a *hot* desert, while Antarctica is a *cold* desert. Antarctica actually receives very little snow, with some areas only getting about two inches of precipitation per year. The Sahara Desert gets about three inches of rain per year. The fact that Antarctica is a desert seems especially strange since it is covered by seven million cubic miles of frozen water! About seventy percent of Earth's fresh water is trapped within Antarctica's ice.

Very Different Deserts

Sahara Desert
- Average temperatures between 80° F and 125° F
- About the size of the United States
- Located on the equator

- Desert regions
- Receive less than 3 inches of rain per year
- Too dry for most plants and animals to live

Antarctica
- Average temperatures between 14° F and -22° F
- 1.5 times larger than the United States
- Located at the South Pole

Antarctic Plants and Animals

There are long periods of time in Antarctica with no sunshine at all, so many plants that need sunlight to make their food would never survive there. However, there are some plant species that need little-to-no light to survive. Small plants such as lichens, algae, and fungi grow on Antarctica's frozen ground. These types of plants feed off decaying plants and animals. This allows them to live in places where other plants can't.

Many different kinds of animals call Antarctica home. Polar bears, penguins, whales, and fish live in Antarctic seas. The polar bear has a thick layer of fat to keep it warm in the freezing temperatures. The male emperor penguin spends the cold Antarctic winter on the ice, balancing his mate's egg on his feet to prevent it from touching the ice and freezing.

Adult whales have thick hides that protect them from the cold ocean waters, but newborn whales would never survive the extreme temperatures. Therefore, the whales will travel north to warmer waters to give birth. When the baby whales are ready, the family travels back home to Antarctica.

Polar bears and emperor penguins spend a lot of time on the ice, so they stand on their heels and point their toes up in the air. That way there's as little as possible touching the ice.

Heading North

The Arctic, or North Pole, is at the northern tip of the planet. It is warmer than Antarctica, but it is still an extreme climate. Antarctica lies at a higher elevation than the Arctic, and higher elevations are usually much colder than lower elevations—think of snow-capped mountains versus sunny beaches. There is actual land beneath Antarctica's ice, but the "land" found in the Arctic is only a floating ice cap between six and ten feet thick. This is why Antarctica is considered a continent, but the Arctic is not.

The waters of the Arctic Ocean, though chilly, are slightly warmer than the ice floating on top of them. Some of this heat passes through the ice and warms the air. However, the North Pole is still a pretty cold place, with winter temperatures averaging -31° F.

The center of the North Pole always stays frozen, but during the winter, more of the ocean freezes, and the Arctic ice cap grows in size. As summer approaches, the ice melts, and the cap shrinks. However, in recent years the Arctic ice cap has been smaller than usual, even in winter. Scientists are concerned that the melting ice cap might mean danger for the people and animals that live in the Arctic. It might also affect weather in other areas by warming the atmosphere and changing wind patterns across the world.

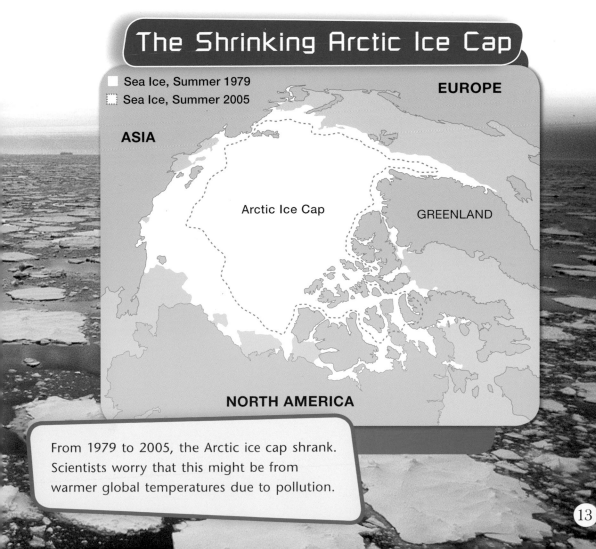

The Shrinking Arctic Ice Cap

Sea Ice, Summer 1979
Sea Ice, Summer 2005

EUROPE

ASIA

Arctic Ice Cap

GREENLAND

NORTH AMERICA

From 1979 to 2005, the Arctic ice cap shrank. Scientists worry that this might be from warmer global temperatures due to pollution.

Tundra plants, which include mosses, lichens, and short shrubs, must be able to survive the freezing conditions. One type of moss, found deep in Siberia's permafrost, stayed alive despite having been frozen for 40,000 years!

South of the Arctic ice cap lies the Arctic tundra, an area with no trees where the ground is always frozen. This tundra includes the northern parts of North America, Europe, and Asia. It has only one month during the year where the temperature is above freezing, and its average temperature is never above 50° F.

Tundra areas can be swampy in the summer despite the fact that they get little rainfall. The Arctic tundra soil has a thick layer of permafrost beneath the surface. Permafrost is a layer of soil underground with a temperature that is always below freezing. When temperatures rise, the top layer of soil thaws out, but because the melted water can't sink into the frozen permafrost, a swampy soil forms that can last all summer.

The Arctic tundra is home to a variety of animals, some of which, such as the grouse and Arctic foxes, turn white during the winter so that they can blend in with the ice. Polar bears usually live on the southern edges of the Arctic ice and in areas even further south, but some have been spotted up near the North Pole. Other Arctic animals include weasels, foxes, lemmings, wolves, musk oxen, reindeer, and caribou.

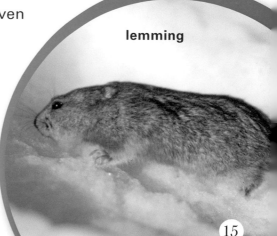

lemming

Chapter 2

The Driest Desert

Fill up your water bottles because we're heading off to another desert. As we learned in the last chapter, a desert can be blistering hot like the Sahara Desert, or it can be freezing cold like Antarctica. Hot or cold, the thing they both have in common is the small amount of rainfall they get.

Land of No Rain

The driest place in the world is the Atacama Desert in the country of Chile, South America. The Atacama Desert is a cool desert—in temperature, that is. Its temperature ranges between 32° F and 73° F, and some parts haven't seen rain for hundreds of years. The Atacama Desert is so extreme that some areas are the only places on Earth where no life can be found—not even tiny bacteria such as those that are able to survive Antarctica's cold.

The long, narrow Atacama Desert stretches up the west coast of South America between the Pacific Ocean and the Andes Mountains. It may seem strange that a desert could be so close to the ocean, but the coastal mountains block moisture from moving inland, while at the same time, the Andes Mountains prevent westward-traveling storms from reaching the dry desert soils.

Parts of the Atacama Desert are flat and rocky, but other areas look more like the surface of the moon. In fact, one area is even named "Valley of the Moon."

Andes Mountains

SOUTH AMERICA

Atacama Desert

CHILE

ATLANTIC OCEAN

N
W   E
S

Scientists are interested in the Atacama Desert's environment because in some ways it is similar to another dry environment—the planet Mars. By studying Atacama's harsh climate, scientists hope to find out just how much water living things need and to learn the best ways to search Mars for signs of life.

Paleontologists, scientists who study the history of ancient human beings, are learning things from the Atacama Desert, too. Because of the dry conditions and lack of bacteria that break down dead plants and animals, dead bodies buried in the desert's sands can turn into well-preserved mummies, some of which are thousands of years old. By studying these mummies, paleontologists learn things about ancient people's diets, cultures, and way of life.

More than a million people live in the Atacama Desert by adapting to the harsh desert climate. They make their homes in coastal villages where the plants get their water from fog instead of from the ground or from rain. In one of these villages, people actually collect the fog and use it to grow food. They cover their crops with nets. The fog condenses on the nets, collects into water droplets, and then drips onto the plants.

This mummy of a young girl is several thousand years old. The Egyptians used salt and chemicals to make their mummies, but since there is very little bacteria in the Atacama Desert, this is a nature–made mummy.

19

Hot Spots

Get out your hat and sunscreen because it's time to find the hottest spots on Earth. You may think they would be located on the equator, where the sun's rays shine directly on Earth's surface, but moisture in the air, clouds, and heavy rainfall keep this area cooler than you might expect. After the warm air over the equator rises and releases its moisture as rain, it is forced on to regions to the north and south, where it heats up to even warmer temperatures.

To see Earth's real hot spots, we'll need to visit the places heated by this stream of warm, dry air. They include the Sahara Desert and Dallol in Africa and Death Valley in the United States.

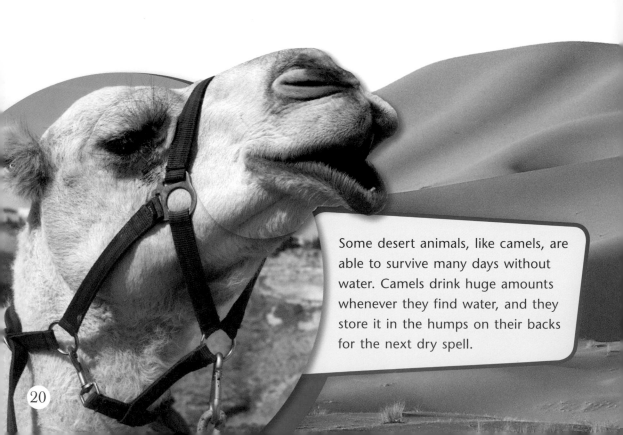

Some desert animals, like camels, are able to survive many days without water. Camels drink huge amounts whenever they find water, and they store it in the humps on their backs for the next dry spell.

Life in the Deep Desert

These three deserts get very little rain, yet animals and plants still manage to survive their harsh environments. Many desert animals are nocturnal, which means they sleep during the day's heat and come out to hunt and eat at night when it's cooler.

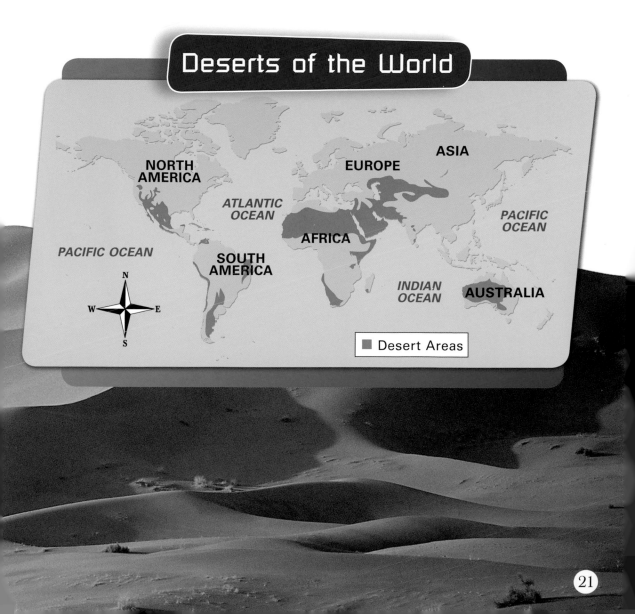

Deserts of the World

NORTH AMERICA

SOUTH AMERICA

EUROPE

ASIA

AFRICA

AUSTRALIA

ATLANTIC OCEAN

PACIFIC OCEAN

PACIFIC OCEAN

INDIAN OCEAN

N
W E
S

■ Desert Areas

scorpion

Many kinds of plants have also found ways to thrive in the hot, dry desert climate. Some plants have long roots that reach deep into the soil to find hidden underground water sources, and other plants have leaves that draw moisture from the air.

A desert oasis is a place where water below the ground comes close enough to the surface where plants can reach it. An oasis is a welcome island of green found in the middle of dry soil and sand, and it provides water for a wide variety of plant and animal life. Caravans, which are large groups of people traveling together, must go from oasis to oasis on their journey through the desert so they can refill their water supplies.

Sahara
Desert

AFRICA

ATLANTIC
OCEAN

World Record Heat

The enormous Sahara Desert in northern
Africa covers an area of more than 3 million
square miles, making it nearly as large as
the entire United States. Shifting sand dunes
blanket about 25 percent of the Sahara, and
gravel-covered plains make up the rest. The
hottest temperature ever recorded anywhere
was at Al Aziziyah, Libya, on the northern
edge of the Sahara Desert. On September 13,
1922, it reached a deadly 136° F!

Salt of the Earth

Badwater, in California's Death Valley, is an area of desert at 282 feet *below* sea level. It's the lowest point in the United States.

Badwater is a salt flat, and at first glance, its surface appears to be covered with a layer of crunchy snow—very unlikely in the hottest place in the country! That white coating is actually a layer of salt left over from thousands of years ago when a lake covered Death Valley. As the lake evaporated, it left behind a salt pan, which is a crust of minerals that was once mixed in with the water.

Death Valley is similar to the Atacama Desert in that a nearby mountain range keeps it very hot and dry. Moisture-filled air from California's coast blows inland to the Sierra Nevada Mountains, which stand to the west of Death Valley. As the air blows up the mountain slopes, it cools off. Cool air can't hold as much water as warm air, so the clouds drop most of their rain or snow on the mountains before they reach Death Valley.

California's Death Valley comes very close to beating Al Aziziyah's record for blistering heat. In 1913 Death Valley reached a temperature of 134° F, and that was in the shade!

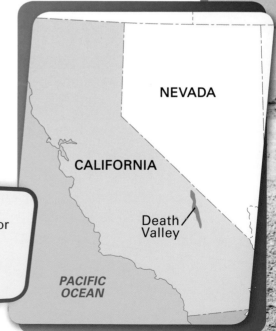

NEVADA

CALIFORNIA

Death Valley

PACIFIC OCEAN

BADWATER

280 FEET/85 METERS

BELOW SEA LEVEL

The Hottest Hot Spot

Many scientists think the hottest place in the world is Dallol in the African country of Ethiopia. Dallol's daytime temperatures during the summer never drop below 104° F. Both day and night temperatures are used to figure out an area's average temperature, and Dallol's average temperature is the highest on Earth—a blistering 93° F.

RED SEA

•Dallol

ETHIOPIA

☐ Dallol Salt Pan

The Dallol region, like Badwater in Death Valley, is a big salt pan, and the ground is crusted with minerals. In the Dallol salt pan, boiling water spurts from the ground, and mustard-colored towers rise like sandcastles on a beach. Many volcanoes are scattered across the region, and their heat forces water up through the layers of minerals. The water quickly evaporates in the hot air, leaving colorful mineral mounds dotting the landscape.

The Afar people live in the Dallol region, and they capture water from the hot springs by building rock domes above them. The vapor from the boiling water condenses on the rocks and then runs down the sides of the domes and into bowls where the people collect it.

Bright green ponds with blooms of sun-colored bacteria make you wonder if you are still on planet Earth!

Water, Water Everywhere

After the heat and dryness of the Sahara, Death Valley, and Dallol, it's time to go looking for water—lots of water. Some of the world's wettest places lie around the equator and in the country of India in southern Asia.

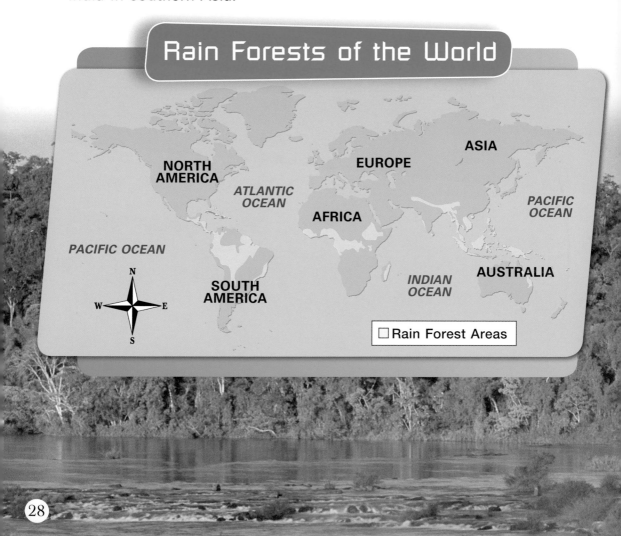

Rain Forests of the World

NORTH AMERICA

EUROPE

ASIA

ATLANTIC OCEAN

AFRICA

PACIFIC OCEAN

PACIFIC OCEAN

SOUTH AMERICA

INDIAN OCEAN

AUSTRALIA

N W E S

☐ Rain Forest Areas

Life in the Rain Forest

The equator's dense tropical rain forests wrap around the planet like a belt of green. With their leafy forest trees and huge variety of life, these rain forests look completely different from the baked desert landscapes we visited in the last chapter.

It's always warm and wet in tropical rain forests, where 70 to 100 inches of rain per year are common. The humidity is also very high in the rain forests, which means that the air contains a lot of moisture. Average temperatures in tropical rain forests range between 68° F and 84° F throughout the year. This may not sound very hot, but with the damp air and so many trees around to block the wind, rain forests often feel hotter than places with higher temperatures and drier air.

Rain forests not only look different from the deserts we've seen so far, they sound different, too—insect clicks, frog croaks, monkey chatter, and bird chirps drift through the hot, sticky air.

Very little sunlight reaches the rain forest floor. Clouds block some of the sunlight, and the leaves of the thick forest trees block almost all of the rest.

More than half of the world's plants and animals live in tropical rain forests, even though the rain forests take up less than five percent of Earth's land surface. Most animals live up in the canopy, the top layer of tree branches, leaves, and vines in a forest. The canopy of the tallest trees grows to more than 160 feet tall.

Although there is an abundance of rain that falls in the rain forest, some plants still don't get the water and nutrients they need. Plants need water to grow, and rain forests certainly get plenty of rain. But many of the larger plants absorb most of the rain before it gets to the smaller plants closer to the ground. Also, there are so many different plant species that nutrients in the soil are used up quickly. Plants need nutrients to stay strong and healthy. Because the large number of plants eat up so many nutrients, many rain forest soils are actually hard places for plants to grow.

Over a million different species of insects live in the world's rain forests. Grasshoppers such as this use their green color to blend in with the background plants.

Some rain forest plants have found a way to solve this problem. Their roots grow high in the top layers of the soil, rather than deep in the ground. These plants get the nutrients first. Plants with shallow roots also collect the nutrients that are released when dead leaves, branches, and fruits fall to the forest floor and rot.

ASIA

INDIA

● Cherrapunji

INDIAN OCEAN

Home of the Clouds

The town of Cherrapunji sits high in India's Khasi Hills in the state of Meghalaya, a name which means "home of the clouds." If you were to drive up to Cherrapunji during winter, you could find yourself behind a row of tanker trucks hauling water to sell on the mountain. This wouldn't be odd if Cherrapunji were a desert—but it's actually one of the wettest spots on Earth!

You might think Cherrapunji would have year-round rainfall, but almost all of the rain falls in the summer months. This leaves the winters so dry that some villagers travel almost a mile to a stream where they can fill empty cans with water.

Cherrapunji receives about 450 inches of rain per year. In July of 1861, it set a record for most rain anywhere in one month—366 inches!

Cherrapunji's rainy season is caused by monsoons, winds that sweep over much of India during July and August and bring heavy rain. Monsoons are caused by the winds changing direction each season. The northeast winds that blow for up to nine months out of the year bring warm, dry winds. Then the winds change direction. Strong, southwest winds bring humid, rainy weather to India.

During India's summer, both the land and the air above the land heat up, but the air that's above the Indian Ocean stays cooler. The warm air rises, and the cooler winds from the ocean rush in to take the warm air's place.

These cooler winds from the Indian Ocean are full of moisture, and as they collide with the Khasi Hills, the winds travel upward, cooling as they go. Cool air can't hold as much water as warm air, so rain falls onto Cherrapunji and other nearby areas.

During the winter, the monsoon direction changes back, and the cool, dry air from the land rushes back out to the ocean. The people who live in Cherrapunji go back to buying water or getting it from streams, and waiting for the next rainy season.

India's Seasonal Winds

Monsoon Season

INDIA

INDIAN
OCEAN

Dry Season

INDIA

INDIAN
OCEAN

During India's monsoon season, cool winds blow inland, bringing heavy monsoon rains. During the dry season, the winds change direction and blow out to sea until the next summer.

Chapter 5

The World's Worst Climate?

Hang onto your hats—we're climbing up a mountain to get a taste of the worst climates in the world. You might think this award should go to the sub-freezing Antarctica, sweltering Dallol, or soggy Cherrapunji. But many scientists believe that Mount Washington, a peak located in the state of New Hampshire, has the world's cruelest climate.

Wild Winds

Mount Washington lies high up in the White Mountains. Its rocky peak stretches 6,288 feet into the sky, making it the highest spot in New England. There is a weather observatory located at the top of the mountain, and the people who live and work there get a first-hand look at some pretty wild weather. It snows more than 250 inches per year. It even snows in July! The average yearly temperature is below freezing. Clouds surround the top of Mount Washington for 60 percent of the year, and for more than 300 days each year, fog rolls in for at least part of the day.

Even though Mount Washington is known for its bad weather, it is still a popular hiking area for tourists eager to challenge themselves on the mountain's windy cliffs.

CANADA

VERMONT

MAINE

Mt. Washington

NEW

MASSACHUSETTS

However, Mount Washington is best known for its fierce winds. In April of 1934, the wind blew at 231 miles per hour and set a world record that has yet to be broken.

Record-breaking Winds

How fast is 231 miles per hour? At wind speeds of 30 miles per hour, it's hard to keep control of an umbrella, and when winds blow 45 miles per hour, it can be difficult for a person to walk. Anything more than 75 miles per hour is considered a hurricane-force wind—and Mount Washington sees 75-mile-per-hour winds an average of 104 days every year!

Mount Washington's height and location give it a place in the weather record books. It isn't especially tall for a mountain, since there are many peaks twice as tall in the Rocky Mountains in Colorado and in the Himalayan Mountains in India. However, Mount Washington is taller than any of the mountains nearby, so the other peaks don't block the wind. Wind increases speed as it travels up a mountain, and by the time it gets to the top, the wind is blowing much faster than it was at the bottom.

Mount Washington sits in a place where winds from several different areas blow towards it. If the mountain were in another part of the country, it wouldn't be so windy.

Life at the Weather Station

Several people—and one pet cat—live in Mount Washington's weather station. Every hour one person goes outside to take weather measurements, unless it's so windy or icy that going out would be dangerous. The scientists send the information they collect to the National Weather Service, which uses the information to help make educated guesses about what the weather for the area will be.

The staff must also clear rime ice off the observatory's instruments. Rime ice is ice that forms in feathery sheets when very cold water vapor freezes to a cold surface. At Mount Washington's weather station, rime ice can grow at a rate of one foot every hour!

The road to the top of Mount Washington is closed to visitors during the winter, but in summer many tourists hike or drive to the top. Signs warn them to turn back if the weather is bad, but many people still brave the trip to the mountaintop to see the amazing views and to buy t-shirts saying they've survived one of the worst climates in the world.

Because the winds on this mountain are so strong, many of the Mount Washington Observatory's buildings have to be chained down. A thin layer of rime ice coats the observatory white for much of the year.

41

Chapter 6 Under the Sea

It's time to leave the canteen and parka behind. We'll need a heavy-duty submarine to get where we're going next. Perhaps the most extreme climate of all can be found not on land, but more than a mile below the ocean's surface.

Deep sea vents on the ocean floor spew blistering soups of chemicals into the cold ocean waters, sort of like small, underwater volcanoes. A long chain of undersea mountains, called the Mid-oceanic Ridge, weaves between the continents, and sea vents are often found near their peaks. The strange creatures that live near the vents are able to survive the darkness and tons of crushing water pushing down upon them.

chemical cloud

Deep sea vents are places where extremely hot water and chemicals come out of the Earth's crust.

sea vent

Sea vents form when seawater seeps down into cracks in the ocean floor and is heated by super-hot magma to temperatures as high as 760° F. The water picks up chemicals from the Earth's crust, then it's forced back up through the ocean floor. The water spouting from the vents can look black or white depending on the chemicals it has collected. This is why some sea vents are called either "black smokers" or "white smokers."

The Mid-oceanic Ridge

The ocean floor is not one solid layer but enormous slabs of rock called tectonic plates. A long line of mountains form along the border where these plates meet, weaving in a jagged line all around the globe. This line of mountains is called the Mid-oceanic Ridge, and it's the longest mountain range in the world, stretching over 37,000 miles.

Along this cracked area in ocean floor is where you find sea vents and all the strange creatures that live near them.

NORTH AMERICA

EUROPE

ASIA

ATLANTIC OCEAN

PACIFIC OCEAN

AFRICA

PACIFIC OCEAN

SOUTH AMERICA

INDIAN OCEAN

AUSTRALIA

N
W E
S

tectonic plate border

Life at a Sea Vent

Although the water coming from these smokers is very, very hot, the surrounding seawater is usually a chilly 35° F to 37° F. As the vent water meets the seawater, its temperature drops hundreds of degrees in the space of only about 6 feet! Imagine if a freezing ice storm and a blistering desert were right next to each other and you could move between them with a single step. That might actually be only a temperature difference of 100° F, while the temperature changes near vents can be many times that.

The tiny animals that live near the smokers are interesting because they don't need energy from the sun the way other plants and animals do. Most plants need the sun's light to make food, and nearly all of Earth's animals either eat plants or eat other animals that eat plants. But the bacteria that live near the sea vents don't need the sun at all. They make energy from the vent water's chemicals, which are poisonous to humans and most other life.

Some of the strangest creatures imaginable have been found in the permanent-dark of the deep, deep ocean. Amazingly, they are able to live without ever seeing the sun.

These sea vent bacteria are at the bottom of the food chain, which means that other animals depend on them to survive. Some animals eat the bacteria themselves, and others eat the animals that eat the bacteria. Giant tubeworms that live near the vents let the bacteria live in their bodies in exchange for the food the bacteria make. It's almost like having your own personal chef!

Giant tubeworms do not have mouths or stomachs. They feed on the bacteria that grow inside of them. These bacteria feed on the chemicals from the sea vents.

The Journey Ends

On our extreme climate tour, we've traveled from the poles to the equator and from tall mountain peaks to deep under the oceans. We've seen some of the hottest, driest, coldest, wettest, windiest, and weirdest places on Earth. Now it's time to head home and be grateful we don't live in the frozen wastelands or lifeless deserts. The world's extreme climates are interesting—but it's *extremely* nice to be home!

Index